D1111136

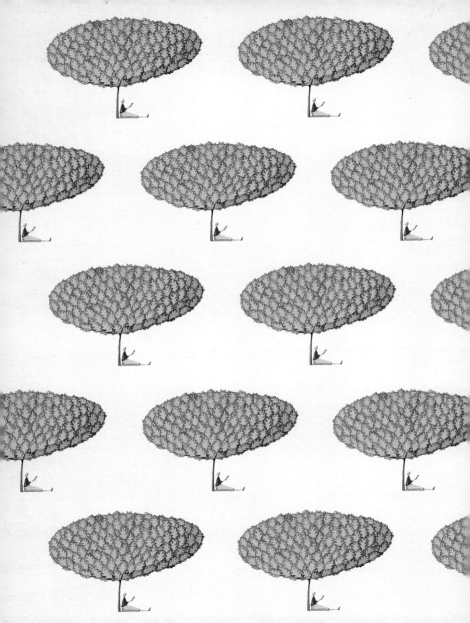

Laura Stoddart trained at Brighton College of Art, where she was commissioned to design the 1996 Christmas stamps for the Royal Mail, the youngest artist ever to receive this prestigious commission. Her work has appeared in *World of Interiors*, *Gardens Illustrated*, *Vogue Entertaining* and other magazines, and on packaging, greetings cards, giftwrap and stationery.

Up the Garden Path

By Laura Stoddart

LAURA STODDART

Up the Garden Path

To my mother for the pictures
And my father for the words

An Orion paperback

First published in Great Britain in 1999
by Orion
This paperback edition published in 2000
by Orion Books Ltd,
Orion House, 5 Upper St Martin's Lane,
London WC2H 9EA

An Hachette Livre UK company

7 9 10 8 6

Reissued 2008

A CIP catalogue record for this book is available
from the British Library.

ISBN 978-0-7528-5813-5

Printed and bound in Italy

The Orion Publishing Group's policy is to use papers that
are natural, renewable and recyclable products and
made from wood grown in sustainable forests. The logging
and manufacturing processes are expected to conform to
the environmental regulations of the country of origin.

www.orionbooks.co.uk

CONTENTS

Go, little book, and wish to all,
Flowers in the garden, meat in the hall,
A bin of wine, a spice of wit,
A house with lawns enclosing it,
A living river by the door,
A nightingale in the sycamore!

Robert Louis Stevenson (1850–1894)

THE HOUSE
Part I

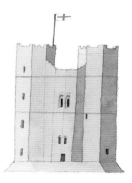
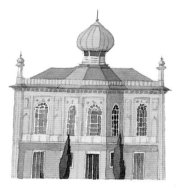

Then we have winding paths, to make butcher-boys
giddy, and perplex the stranger . . . and which compel
the visitor to make half a tour of the grounds, when
his chief object is to get inside the house, to take off
his hat and gloves, and sit at the table punctual to a
moment. Depend upon it, the best taste for an
approach to a house is to have it as direct as possible.

Shirley Hibberd (1825–1890) *The Town Garden*

3

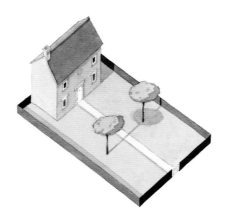

We are born at home, live at home,
and we must die at home, so that the
comfort and economy of home are of
more deep, heartfelt and personal
interest to us, than the public affairs of
all the nations of the world.

Motto of *The Magazine of Domestic Economy*, 1835

Be it ever so humbug, there's no place
like home.

Noel Coward (1899–1973)

Home is where you go to when you've
nowhere to go.

Bette Davis (1908–1959)

By all accounts, 'tis very fine,
But where d'ye sleep, and where d'ye
dine?
I find by all you have been telling
That 'tis a house, but not a dwelling.

Jonathan Swift (1667–1745) from *Verses on Blenheim*

A sofa is a piece of furniture which affords
a great source of comfort to its possessor.

John Claudius Loudon (1783–1843)

I sing the sofa.

William Cowper (1730–1800) from *The Task*

It was an armchair that was my undoing.

Madame Elizabeth, daughter of Louis XIV,
when asked why she did not become a nun

I had three chairs in my house: one for solitude,
two for friendship, three for society.

H. D. Thoreau (1817–1862) from *Walden*

A rickety chair will not serve as a seat.

Anonymous

I should like the window to open on to the lake of
Geneva – and there I'd sit and read all day like the
picture of somebody reading.

John Keats (1795–1821) in a letter to his sister, Fanny

Dreams, books, are each a world; and books, we know,
Are a substantial world, both pure and good.
Round these, with tendrils strong as flesh and blood,
Our pastime and our happiness will grow.

William Wordsworth (1770–1850) from *Personal Talk*

People say that life is the thing, but I prefer books.

Logan Pearsall Smith (1865–1946) from *Afterthoughts* 1931

(There is) no furniture so charming as books, even if
you never open them, or read a single word.

Sydney Smith (1771–1845)

The landscape from an eating room is of less consequence than any other.

John Claudius Loudon (1783–1843)

He may live without books, – what is knowledge but grieving?
He may live without hope, – what is hope but deceiving?
He may live without love, – what is passion but pining?
But where is the man that can live without dining?

Edward Robert Bulwer, Earl of Lytton, from *Lucile*, 1860

If the soup had been as warm as the wine, and
the wine as old as the fish, and the fish as young
as the maid, and the maid as willing as the hostess,
it would have been a very good meal.

Anonymous

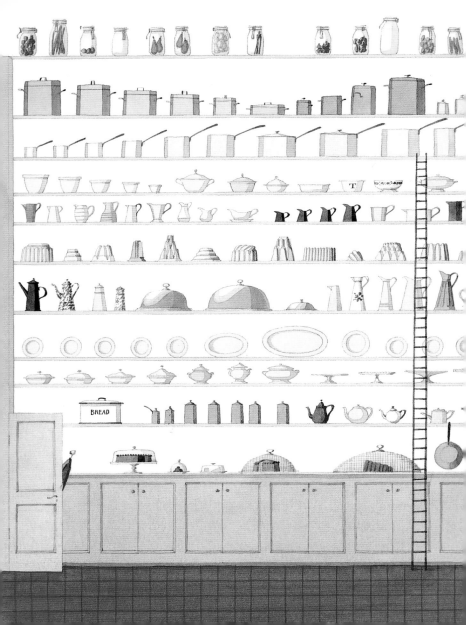

I saw him even now going the way of all flesh,
that is to say towards the kitchen.

John Webster (1580–1625) *Westward Hoe*

The kitchen is a country in which there are always
discoveries to be made.

Grimod de la Regnière

We may live without poetry, music and art;
We may live without conscience, and live without heart;
We may live without friends; we may live without books;
But civilized man cannot live without cooks.

Edward Robert Bulwer, Earl of Lytton, from *Lucile*, 1860

Kissing don't last, cookery do!

George Meredith (1828–1909) from *The Ordeal of Richard Feverel*

What is literature compared with cooking?
The one is shadow, the other substance.

E. V. Lucas (1868–1938)

Housekeeping ain't no joke!

Louisa May Alcott (1832–1888)

Everyone can keep house better than
her mother till she trieth.

French proverb

Trifles make perfection, but
perfection is no trifle.

Shaker maxim

14

There was no need to do any housework at all. After the first four years the dirt doesn't get any worse.

> Quentin Crisp (b.1908) from *The Naked Civil Servant*

I make no secret of the fact that I would rather lie on a sofa then sweep beneath it.

> Shirley Conran (b.1932) from *The Reason Why*

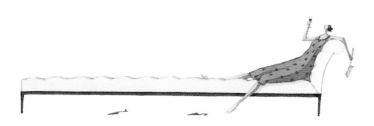

Ethels room was indeed a handsome compartment with purple silk curtains and a 4 post bed draped with the same shade. The toilit set was white and mouve and there were some violets in a costly varse. Oh I say cried Ethel in supprise. I am glad you like it said Bernard and here we have yours Alf. He opened the dividing doors and portrayed a smaller but dainty room all in pale yellow and wild primroses. My own room is next the bath room said Bernard it is decerated dark red as I have somber tastes. The bath room has got a tip up bason and a hose thing for washing your head. A good notion said Mr Salteena who was secretly getting jellus.

Daisy Ashford (aged 9) from *The Young Visiters*, 1919

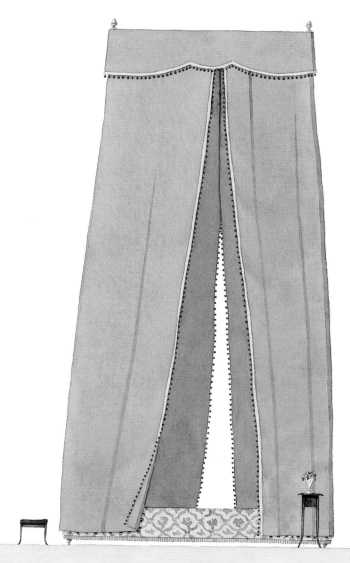

O! it's nice to get up in the morning,
But it's nicer to stay in bed.

Harry Lauder (1870–1950)

For worst or best,
Right good is rest.

Anonymous

No human being believes that any other
human being has a right to be in bed when
he himself is up.

Robert Lynd (1879–1947)

The way to bliss lies not on beds of down.

Anonymous

The deep, deep peace of the double bed
after the hurly-burly of the chaise longue.

Mrs Patrick Campbell (1865–1940)

If your sovereign will to the bath, his body to wash clean,
Hang sheets round about the roof. This is how I mean,
Every sheet full of flowers and herbs sweet and green,
And look you have sponges five or six, thereon to sit or lean.
Look there be a great sponge, thereon your sovereign to sit,
And on it a sheet, so he may bathe him there a fit,
Under his feet also a sponge, if there be any to put,
And always be sure of the door, and see that it is shut.
Take a basin in your hand full of hot herbs and fresh
And with a soft sponge in hand [start] his body to wash.
Rinse him with rose water warm and fair upon his flesh
Then let him go to bed, but see that it's sweet and nesh.
But first set on his socks, his slippers on his feet,
That he may go fair to the fire, there to take his foot sheet,
Then with a clean cloth to wipe away all wet.
Then bring him to his bed, his troubles there to beat.

John Russell, *The Boke of Nurture*, c.1460

Bath twice a day to be really clean, once a day to be
passably clean, once a week to avoid being a public
menace.

Anthony Burgess (1917–1994) *Inside Mr Enderby*

I want a house that has got over all its troubles. I don't want to spend the rest of my life bringing up a young and inexperienced house.

Jerome K. Jerome (1859–1927) from *They and I*

The house discovers the owner.

Randle Cotgrove, 1611

If I were asked to say what is at once the most important production of Art and the thing most longed for, I should answer a beautiful house.

William Morris (1834–1896)

Your house is your larger body.
It grows in the sun and sleeps in the stillness of the night, and it is not dreamless. Does not your house dream? and dreaming, leave the city for grove or hill-top?

Kahlil Gibran (1883–1931) *The Prophet*

THE GARDEN
Part II

God Almightie first planted a Garden. And indeed, it is the Purest of Humane pleasure. It is the Greatest Refreshment to the Spirits of Man.

Francis Bacon (1561–1626) *Essays*

Is the fancy too far brought, that this love for gardens is a
reminiscence haunting the race of that remote time when
but two persons existed – a gardener named Adam and a
gardener's wife called Eve?

Alexander Smith (1830–1867)

(Gardening) is not graceful, and it makes one hot; but
it is a blessed sort of work, and if Eve had had a spade
in Paradise and known what to do with it, we should
not have had all that sad business of the apple.

Elizabeth, Countess von Arnim (1866–1941)

A garden without trees scarcely deserves to be called a garden.

Canon Henry Ellacombe
(1790–1885)

I never before knew the full value of trees. My house is entirely embosomed in high plane trees, with good grass below, and under them I breakfast, dine, write, read and receive my company.

Thomas Jefferson (1743–1826)

Trees are the best monuments that a man can erect to his own memory. They speak his praises without flattery, and they are blessings to children yet unborn.

Lord Orrery (1707–1762)

A lawn, a lily
  And a lilac tree:
They take a lot of beating,
  Wherever they be.

Reginald Arkell (1882–1959) *New Saying*

My garden sweet, enclosed with walles strong,
Enbanked with benches to sytt and take my rest:
The knotts so enknotted, it cannot be exprest,
With arbors and alyes so pleasaunt and so dulce.

George Cavendish (1499–1561)

  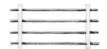

A hedge between keeps friendship green.

Proverb

A low hedge is easily leapt over.

Proverb

Woman has no seductions for the man who cannot keep his eyes off his magnolias.

Anonymous

I'm a broken-hearted gardener and don't know what to do,
My love she is inconstant and a fickle jade too;
One smile from her lips will never be forgot,
It refreshes like a shower from a watering pot.
Oh, Oh! She's a fickle wild rose,
A damask, a cabbage, a young China rose.
She's my myrtle, my geranium,
My sunflower, my sweet marjoram.
My honeysuckle, my tulip, my violet,
My hollyhock, my dahlia,
My little mignonette.

from *The Broken-Hearted Gardener* (a street ballad)

GWENDOLEN Quite a well kept garden this is, Miss Cardew.

CECILY So glad you like it, Miss Fairfax.

GWENDOLEN I had no idea there were any flowers in the country.

CECILY Oh, flowers are as common here, Miss Fairfax, as people are in London.

Oscar Wilde (1854–1900) *The Importance of Being Earnest*

Who loves a garden, loves a greenhouse too.

William Cowper (1731–1800)

How much better, during a long and dreary winter,
for daughters, and even sons, to assist, or attend,
their mother, in a greenhouse, than to be seated
with her at cards, or, in the blubberings over a
stupid novel, or at any other amusement that
can possibly be conceived!

William Cobbett (1763–1835)

You buy some flowers for your table;
You tend them tenderly as you're able;
You fetch them water from hither and thither –
What do you get for it all? They wither.

Samuel Hoffenstein (1890–1947)

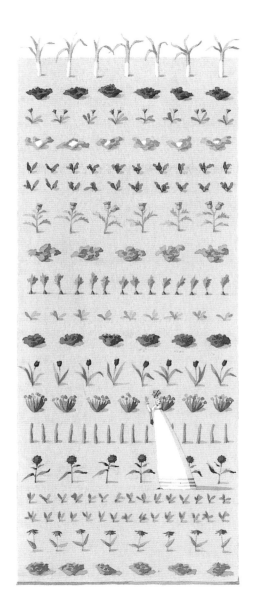

Can the garden afford anything more delightful to view than those forests of asparagus, artichokes, lettuce, peas, beans and other legumes and edulous plants so different in colour and of such various shapes, rising as it were from the dead and piercing the ground in so many thousand places as they do, courting the admiration or requiring the care of the diligent.

Stephen Switzer (1682–1745) *The Practical Gardiner*

They were out when we came. I rushed to the potager – you know my weakness – and walked up and down between spinach and dahlias in ecstasy.

Harriet, Countess Granville, 1828

Who can endure a Cabbage Bed in October?

Jane Austen (1775–1817)

Even the clipt yews interest me; and if I found one in any garden that should be mine, in the shape of a peacock, I should be as proud to keep his tail well spread as the man who first carved him.

Robert Southey (1774–1843)

Our trees rise in cones, globes and pyramids. We see the marks of the scissors upon every plant and bush . . . I would rather look upon a tree in all its luxuriancy and diffusion of boughs and branches, than when it is thus cut and trimmed into a mathematical figure; and cannot but fancy that an orchard in flower looks infinitely more delightful, than all the little labyrinths of the most finished parterre.

Joseph Addison (1672–1719)

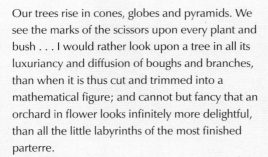

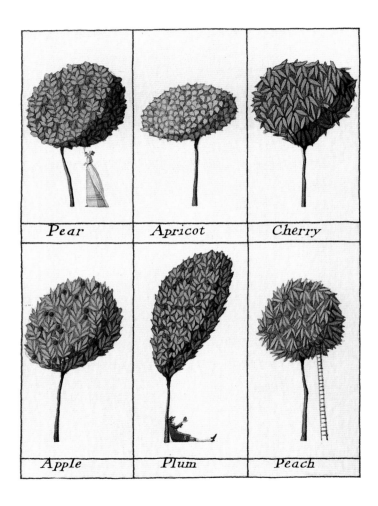

| Pear | Apricot | Cherry |
| Apple | Plum | Peach |

What can your eye desire to see, your ears to hear,
your mouth to take, or your nose to smell, that is not
to be had in an orchard, with abundance of variety?

William Lawson, *A New Orchard and Garden*, 1618

I like to think how Shakespeare pruned his rose,
And ate his pippin in his orchard close.

William Rose Benét (1886–1950)

An apple tree puts to shame all the men and women
that have attempted to dress since the world began.

H. M. Beecher (1813–1887)

Fair pledges of a fruitful tree,
Why do ye fall so fast?

Robert Herrick (1591–1674) from *Hesperides*

In fine weather the old gentleman is almost constantly in the garden; and when it is too wet to go into it, he will look out of the window at it by the hour together. He has always something to do there, and you will see him digging, and sweeping, and cutting, and planting, with manifest delight . . . ; and in the evening when the sun has gone down, the perseverance with which he lugs a great watering-pot about is perfectly astonishing.

Charles Dickens (1812–1870) *Sketches by Boz*

Did you ever meet a gardener, who, however fair his ground, was absolutely content and pleased? . . . Is there not always a tree to be felled or a bed to be turfed? . . . Is there not ever some grand mistake to be remedied next summer?

The Rev. Samuel Hole (1819–1904)

Some ladies asked me why their plant had died.
They had got it from the very best place, and they
were sure they had done their very best for it . . .
They had made a nice hole with their new trowel,
and for its sole benefit they had bought a tin of
Concentrated Fertilizer. This they had emptied into
the hole, put in the plant, and covered it up and
given it lots of water, and – it had died! And yet
these were the best and kindest of women, who
would never have dreamed of feeding a new-born
infant on beefsteaks and raw brandy.

Gertrude Jekyll (1843–1932) from *Wood and Garden*

A gardener's work is never at an end.

John Evelyn (1620–1706) from *Kalendarium Hortense*

GARDEN GEAR AT HOLKHAM, 1761

In the Pleasure Grounds and Orangery

20 Barrow Chairs
3 Double Seated Chairs
20 Small Winsor Chairs
6 Compass Back Chairs

Plants and Trees in Tubs and Pots

250 Pines in Pots [pineapples]
4 Citrons in Tubs
46 Orange Trees in Tubs
9 Lemon Trees in Pots
3 Broad Leafed Myrtles in Tubs

25 Double and Single Leafed Myrtles in Pots
70 Seedling Oranges in Pots
13 Aloes in Pots

Working Tools and Utensils

11 Scythes
6 Rakes
5 Dutch Hoes
8 English Hoes
8 Forks
3 Jets
6 Watering Pots
2 Tin Pipes for Watering Pines
1 House Engine
1 Brass Hand Engine
2 Wooden Hand Engines [all for water]
3 Leather Pipes
1 Suction Pipe
1 Brass Pipe
1 Rose [for sprinkling]
2 Thermometers
2 Shovels
4 Hammers
1 Hook [Sickle]
1 Hatchet
2 Iron Rollers
5 Boots for Horses to Roller the Garden with
8 Hand Basket for Fruit

1 Pair of Garden Shears
1 Mallet and Pruning Chisel
2 Mattocks
1 Flag Shovel
1 Edging Tool
2 Pair of Iron Reels with Lines
2 Hand Saws
1 Grindstone and Frame
4 Rubstones
1 Cucumber cutter
91 Frames Glazed for Melons Pines and Cucumbers
35 Frames for the Fire Walls
21 Hand Glasses
9 Bell Glasses
    Netting in five Parcels
    A Number of Old Mats
8 Common Wheel Barrows
2 Water Barrows
3 Water Tubs
3 Stone Rollers
1 Large Fruit Basket
8 Bushell Baskets
3 Water Pails
    INVENTORY Holkham MSS

47

What a man needs in gardening is a cast-iron back
with a hinge in it.

Charles Dudley Warner (1829–1900)

The best way to get real enjoyment out of the garden is
to put on a wide straw hat, hold a little trowel in one
hand and a cool drink in the other, and tell the man
where to dig.

Charles Barr

Oh, Adam was a gardener, and God who made him sees
That half a proper gardener's work is done upon his knees.

Rudyard Kipling (1865–1936) from *The Glory of the Garden*

May I assure the gentleman who writes to me (quite often)
from a Priory in Sussex that I am not the armchair, library-
fireside gardener he evidently suspects . . . and that for the
last forty years of my life I have broken my back, my
fingernails, and sometimes my heart, in the practical pursuit
of my favourite occupation!

Vita Sackville-West (1892–1962)

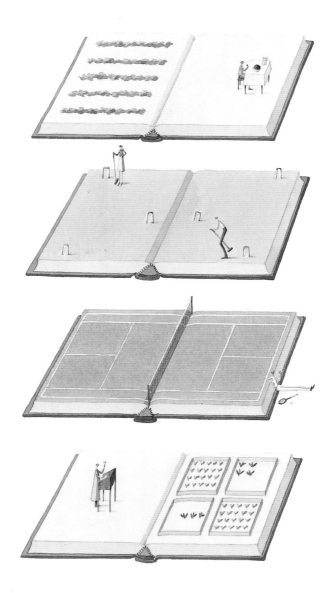

A garden must be looked unto and dressed as the body.

George Herbert (1593–1633)

A modest garden contains, for those who know how to look and to wait, more instruction than a library.

Henri Frédéric Amiel (1821–1881)

I asked a schoolboy, in the sweet summertide, 'what he thought a garden was for?' and he said Strawberries. His younger sister suggested Croquet and the elder Garden-parties. The brother from Oxford made a prompt declaration in favour of Lawn Tennis and Cigarettes, but he was rebuked by a solemn senior ... and was told that 'a garden was designed for botanical research, and for the classification of plants'.

The Rev. Samuel Hole (1819–1904) from *Is He Dead Yet?*

Into your garden you can walk
And with each plant and flower talk;
View all their glories, from each one
Raise some rare meditation.

John Rea from *Flora, Ceres and Pomona*, 1665

It was the morning of the sixth of May,
And May had painted with her soft showers
A garden full of leaves and flowers.
And man's hand had arrayed it with such craft
There never was a garden of such price
But if it were the very Paradise.

Geoffrey Chaucer (1343–1400) from *The Canterbury Tales*

Then in we went, to the garden glorious
Like to a place, of pleasure most solacious
With flora paynted and wrought curiously
In divers knottes of marveylous greatnes.

Anonymous

It is good to be alone in a garden at dawn or dark, so that all its shy presences may haunt you and possess you in a reverie of suspended thought.

James Douglas (1753–1819)

A garden is a delight to the eye, and a solace to the soil; it soothes angry passions, and produces that pleasure which is a foretaste of Paradise.

Sa' Di (1184–1291)

What is a weed? A plant whose virtues have not yet been discovered.

Ralph Waldo Emerson (1803–1882) from *Fortune of the Republic*

A place where the mind goes to seed.

Anonymous

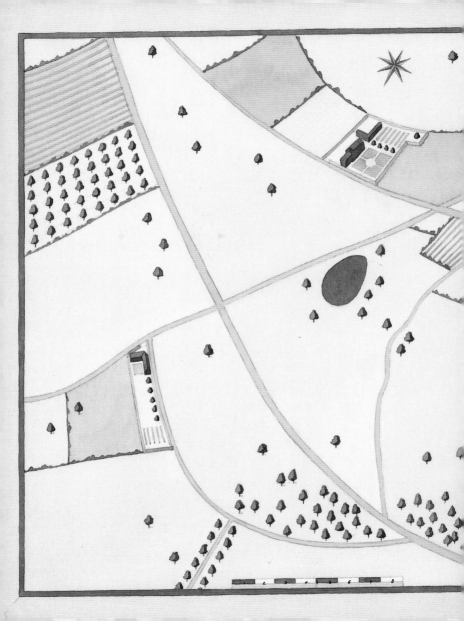

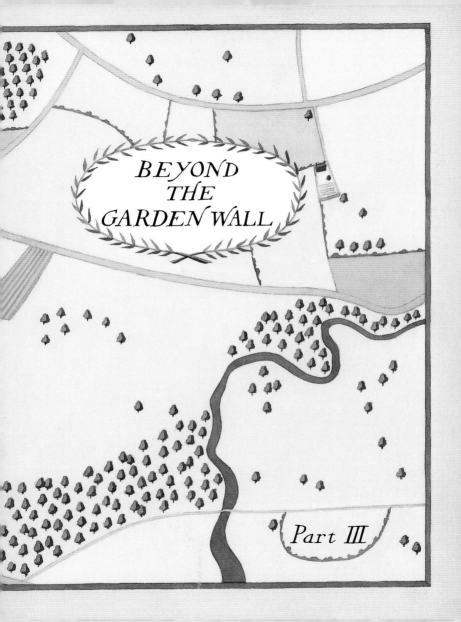

BEYOND
THE
GARDEN WALL

Part III

If we had keen vision and feeling of all ordinary human life, it would be like hearing the grass grow and the squirrel's heart beat, and we should die of that roar which lies on the other side of silence.

George Eliot (1819–1880)

The day, water, sun, moon, night – I do not have to purchase these things with money.

Plautus (c.254–184 B.C.)

In nature everything is distinct, yet nothing defined into absolute independent singleness.

William Wordsworth (1770–1850) from *Guide to the Lakes*

Never does nature say one thing and wisdom another.

Juvenal (c. 55–127A.D.)

At twilight nature becomes a wonderfully suggestive effect, and is not without loveliness, though perhaps its chief use is to illustrate quotations from the poets.

Oscar Wilde (1854–1900)

Nature is all very well, but is a bore when taken neat.

Anthony Blunt (1907–1983)

God made the country, and man made the town.

Anonymous

The Statesman, lawyer, merchant, man of trade,
Pants for the refuge of some rural shade.

William Cowper (1731–1800)

"I shall soon be rested," said Fanny; "to sit in the shade on a fine day, and look upon verdure, is the most perfect refreshment."

Jane Austen (1775–1817) from *Mansfield Park*

Five minutes on even the nicest mountain
Are awfully long.

W. H. Auden (1907–1973) *Mountains*

Gentlemen know that fresh air should be kept in its proper place –
out of doors – and that God having given us indoors and out-of-
doors, we should not attempt to do away with the distinction.

Rose Macaulay (1881–1958)

When two Englishmen meet, their first talk is of the weather.

Samuel Johnson (1709–1784)

Everybody talks about the weather, but nobody
does anything about it.

Charles Dudley Warner (1829–1900)

Summer afternoon – summer afternoon; to me those
have always been the two most beautiful words in
the English language.

Henry James (1843–1916)

What dreadful hot weather we have! It keeps me in
a continual state of inelegance.

Jane Austen (1775–1817)

Thank heavens, the sun has gone in, and I don't have to
go out and enjoy it.

Logan Pearsall Smith (1865–1946) from *All Trivia*

Some are weather-wise, some otherwise.

Benjamin Franklin (1706–1790)

Nature, Mr Allnut, is what we are put into this world to rise above.

From *The African Queen* (screenplay James Agate and John Huston)

When clouds appear like rocks and towers,
The earth's refreshed by frequent showers.

Anonymous

Who has seen the wind?
   Neither you nor I;
But when the trees bow down their heads
   The wind is passing by.

Christina Rossetti (1830–1894) from 'The Wind'

I love snow, and all the forms
    Of the radiant frost;
I love waves, and winds, and storms,
    Everything almost
Which is Nature's, and may be
    Untainted by man's misery.

Percy Bysshe Shelley (1792–1822) from *Rarely, Comest Thou*

... He heard the snow falling through the universe and faintly falling, like the descent of their last end, upon all the living and the dead.

James Joyce (1882–1941) *Dubliners*

Merry and tranquil! Tedious and brief!
That is, hot ice and wondrous strange snow.

> William Shakespeare (1564–1616) *A Midsummer
> Night's Dream*

A white bird featherless floats down through the air
And never a tree but he lights there.

> Riddle

Snow, snow, snow
I want to wash my feet, my hair,
   my hands, and teeth, in snow.

> Anonymous

Water is best.

Pliny (518-437BC)
inscription over the Pump Room, Bath

When we please to walk abroad
For our recreation,
In the fields is our abode,
Full of delectation:
   Where in a Brook
   With a Hook,
   On a Lake
   Fish we take,
   There we sit,
Till we fish entangle.

Izaak Walton (1593–1683) from
The Compleat Angler

I come into the presence of still water. And I
feel above the day-blind stars waiting with their light.

Wendell Berry from *The Peace of Wild Things*, 1968

Water is the eye of a landscape.

Anonymous

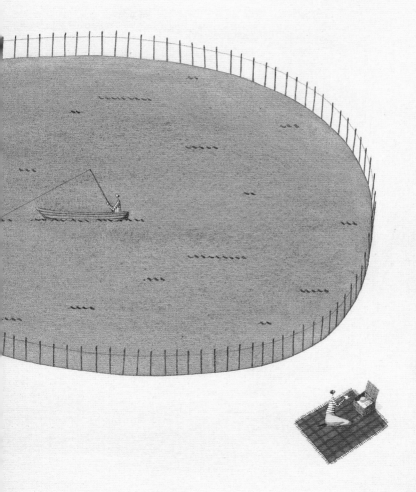

Why are there trees I never walk under but large and melodious thoughts descend upon me?

Walt Whitman (1819–1892)

A solitary maple on a woodside flames in single scarlet, recalling nothing so much as the daughter of a noble house dressed for a fancy ball, with the whole family gathered round to admire her before she goes.

Henry James (1843–1916)

A large, branching oak is perhaps the most
venerable of all inanimate objects.

William Shenstone (1714–1763)

I pray you, mar no more trees with writing love
songs in their barks.

William Shakespeare (1564–1616) from *As You Like It*

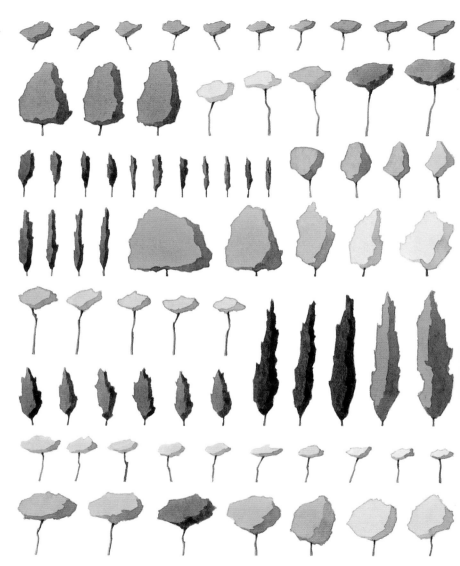

Poems are made by fools like me,
But only God can make a tree.

Joyce Kilmer (1886–1918) from *Trees*

The Oak is called the king of trees,
The Aspen quivers in the breeze,
The Poplar grows up straight and tall,
The Peach tree spreads along the wall,
The Sycamore gives pleasant shade,
The Willow droops in watery glade,
The Fir tree useful timber gives,
The Beech amid the forest lives.

Sara Coleridge (1802–1850) *Trees*

I am for the woods against the world,
but are the woods for me?

Edmund Blunden (1896–1974) from *The Kiss*

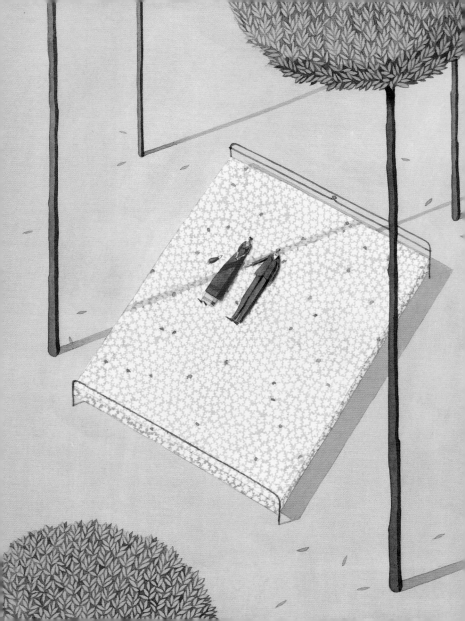

The wood, where often you and I
Upon faint primrose beds were wont to lie.

William Shakespeare (1564–1616)
from *A Midsummer Night's Dream*

Bring hither the pink and the purple columbine,
With gillyflowers:
Bring coronation, and sops in wine,
Worn of paramours:
Strew me the ground with daffadowndillies,
And cowslips, and kingcups, and loved lilies.

Edmund Spenser (1551–1599) from *The Shepheard's Calendar*

To see a World in a Grain of Sand
And a Heaven in a Wild Flower,
Hold Infinity in the palm of your hand
And Eternity in an hour.

William Blake (1757–1827) from *Auguries of Innocence*

To me the meanest flower that blows can give
Thoughts that do often lie too deep for tears.

William Wordsworth (1770–1850)
'Ode: Imitations of Immortality'

Green, I love you green. Green wind.
Green branches

Federico García Lorca (1898–1936)

A child said 'What is the grass?' fetching it to me with
full hands.
How could I answer the child? I do not know what
it is any more than he.

Walt Whitman (1819–1892) from *Leaves of Grass*

I love the English country scene
But sometimes think there's too much Hooker's green,
Especially in August when the flowers that might have lent a
Lightness, don't; being gamboge or magenta.

Stevie Smith (1902–1971) from 'I Love …'

If I keep a green bough in my heart, the singing bird will come.

Anonymous

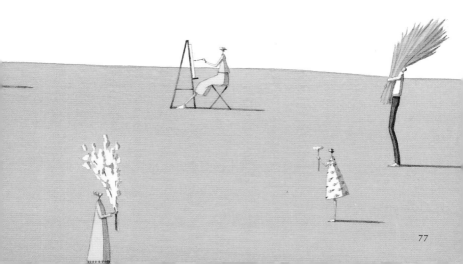

January	*February*	*March*
April	*May*	*June*
July	*August*	*September*
October	*November*	*December*

JANUARY	By this fire I warm my hands.
FEBRUARY	And with my spade I delfe my lands.
MARCH	Here I set my thynge to Spring.
APRIL	And here I hear the fowlis sing.
MAY	I am as light as bird in bough.
JUNE	And I weed my corn well inow.
JULY	With my scythe my mead I mawe.
AUGUST	And here I shear my corn full low.
SEPTEMBER	With my flail I earn my bread.
OCTOBER	And here I sawe my wheat so red.
NOVEMBER	At Martinsmass I kill my swine.
DECEMBER	And at Christemass I drink red wine.

Anonymous

Great Mother, let Me Once be able
To have a Garden, House and Stable;
That I may Read, and Ride, and Plant,
Superior to Desire, or Want;
And as Health fails, and Years increase,
Sit down, and think, and die in peace.

Matthew Prior (1664–1721)

ACKNOWLEDGEMENTS

The compiler and Publisher would like to thank
the following for permission to use copyright
material: Random House UK Ltd for 'The Young
Visiters' by Daisy Ashcroft and for quotations from
Inside Mr Enderby by Anthony Burgess; Addison,
Wesley Longman Ltd for quotations from *Wood
and Green* by Gertrude Jekyll; Curtis Brown on
behalf of The Estate for Vita Sackville-West;
Janklow & Nesbit for quotations from *The Reason
Why* and *Superwoman II* by Shirley Conran. Every
endeavour has been made on the part of the
Publisher to contact copyright holders not
mentioned above and the Publisher will be happy
to include a full acknowledgement in any future
edition.

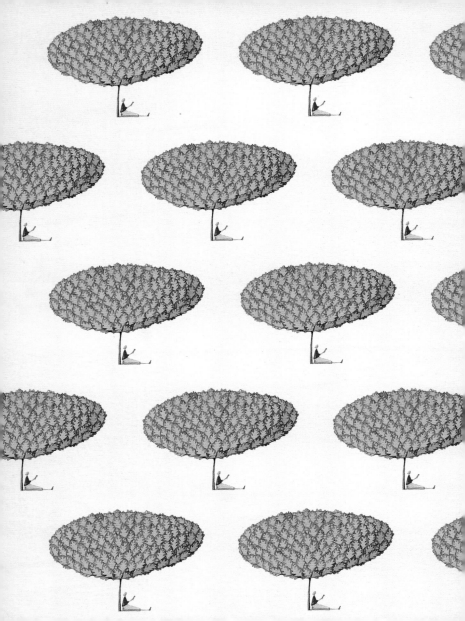